Short Story Writing

Short Story Writing

HERON
BOOKS

lishebooks.cSpecial thanks to all the teachers and students who
provided feedback instrumental to this edition.

Fourth Edition © 1986, 2021 Heron Books
All Rights Reserved

ISBN 978-0-89-739266-2

Any unauthorized copying, translation, duplication or distribution, in whole or in part, by any means,
including electronic copying, storage or transmission, is a violation of applicable laws.

The Heron Books name and the heron bird symbol are registered trademarks
of Delphi Schools, Inc.

Printed in the USA

30 November 2021

At Heron Books, we think learning should be engaging and fun. It should be hands-on and allow students to move at their own pace.

To facilitate this we have created a learning guide that will help any student progress through this book, chapter by chapter, with confidence and interest.

Get learning guides at
heronbooks.com/learningguides.

For teacher resources,
such as a final exam, email
teacherresources@heronbooks.com.

We would love to hear from you!
Email us at *feedback@heronbooks.com.*

Contents

CHAPTER 1

Getting Your
Point Across in Writing

CHAPTER 1

Getting Your
Point Across in Writing

INTRODUCTION

Think of a time when you read a book or a story that you really enjoyed. It is likely that the writer of that book or story was successful in getting a communication across to you.

Think of something else you really enjoyed reading. Think about what communication the writer got across to you.

The most important thing to know about writing is that it is just a form of communication, like talking. Just as you talk to someone else, a good writer writes to someone with the intention of communicating his ideas.

Just as a person grows up and progresses from communicating in simple words and sentences to communicating complex ideas with speech, one can become an accomplished writer with practice.

But why would *you* want to spend a lot of time learning to write better? If you want to become a professional writer, the answer is obvious.

But even if you don't, the answer is still easy. *Writing is one of the best ways of getting yourself and your ideas well known and well thought of.* The ability to get a point across in writing is necessary to get your ideas or viewpoints known.

Just about everybody has a need to communicate in writing to some person. That person may be a boss or an employee, a friend or family member. How well you can do it can affect how well you get along in life.

In business, the ability to produce a good written presentation can make the difference between success and failure. A scientist or inventor who can communicate original ideas in writing has a much better chance of success than one who can't. Getting others to understand your ideas or your viewpoints can be very useful in all parts of life.

There are many things to know about writing, some important, some not so important. If you understand the most fundamental ideas in the subject of writing first, it will be easier to master the rest later.

SOME WRITING FUNDAMENTALS

Writing Is a Communication

Again, the first thing to notice about writing is that it is just a kind of communication. Let's take a closer look at this.

1. It is the writer who is communicating *to the reader.*

   Even when you are writing something required for school, you can still decide to make it a communication that goes from you to the reader.

Have a Message

2. Have something to say—a message.

    The **point** of the writing is the message that a writer wants to get across to a reader. It could be information or an opinion about something. It could be an emotion or feeling. It could be a general attitude or viewpoint. It could be an image, picture, or idea. It could be anything the writer wants the reader to understand.

    It is easy to have a message if you always write about something that interests you. If you are getting ready to research and write about Afghanistan for a story, you may find you're not interested in what you are finding. If so, find something about Afghanistan that does interest you, so you have something to say.

    Start each piece of writing with a message to communicate.

Enough Specifics

3. To get your point across in writing, you usually need to support your general ideas with specifics.

    You have to say enough about your subject to make it real to the reader. Saying enough doesn't necessarily mean using a lot of words. It means giving enough details and specifics to get the reader to understand your point.

    A good writer uses just enough details to make each piece interesting and worth reading.

    This same idea applies to most kinds of non-fiction writing as well. Get a newspaper. Read a new article and notice how the writer uses details to get the point across. Imagine what the story would be like if the author didn't use details. Would you bother to read it?

    To get the reader to see your point, support your point with enough specifics.

Checking Over How Well You Communicated

4. Reread your writing, noting anything that doesn't communicate well. Revise it so the reader receives it as you intended.

   There is one problem with writing that doesn't exist with talking. In writing, your reader can't stop you on the spot to tell you that your writing is hard to understand.

   For example, you're telling a friend that you think helmets should be required for motorcycles. Your friend says, "Oh, come on. Plenty of people ride motorcycles without helmets perfectly safely." As you are very well informed, you give specific examples and the latest figures. Your friend gets your point. But in writing, when you don't make your point, you usually don't get a second chance.

   You can make sure your writing gets the intended point across before giving it to readers. Once you finish a piece, put your writing away for an hour or a day. Then reread it freshly to ensure it communicates exactly what you want.

Proofreading

5. Do your best job of proofreading.

   Mistakes such as misspelled words, strange punctuation, or awkward, unclear sentences can be a real barrier to getting your point across. When you have too many errors, the reader's attention goes off your message and onto the goofs.

   You seldom see errors in magazines and books you read. This is because publishers hire professional proofreaders to find and correct any mistakes so their writing doesn't look bad. Since most writers can't afford to hire professional proofreaders, they learn to find and correct their own mistakes.

Summary

1. As a writer, be communicating *to* somebody.

2. Have a message. Know what point you want to communicate to the reader.

3. Give the reader enough specifics to support your point.

4. Reread and revise your writing to make sure it communicates well. (Set it aside for a while if necessary and then come back to it when you can look at it freshly.)

5. Proofread and do your best to eliminate all errors.

CHAPTER 2

Simple Outlining

CHAPTER 2

Simple Outlining

A simple outline is often the single most helpful tool used in writing a good story. It will help you achieve a unified, organized composition.

Start to outline by listing as many different items as you can think of concerning your topic. Don't worry about putting the list in order.

Here's an example for a story about planting a tulip garden:

Why I like tulips.

Enjoying the flowers in the spring.

Looking at a tulip catalog.

Deciding on colors and types of tulips.

Looking at the garden area and deciding where to plant.

Preparing the soil with fertilizer.

Making sketch of flowerbed showing color patterns.

Figuring out how many bulbs are needed and ordering them.

Describing spring weather in England.

Planting them at the right time in the fall.

Learning the history of tulips.

Snipping off the dead tulips during blooming period.

Why I want a tulip garden.

Then place the items in the order you wish to use for writing your story. There are several ways to do this. You can place the items:

- in order from most to least important,

- in order from least to most important,

- in chronological order, or

- in a combination of time and order of importance.

Then eliminate any unnecessary items from your list.

Perhaps you decide to put this story in chronological order. The rearranged and trimmed list would look like this:

Why I want a tulip garden.

Look at the garden area. Decide on a space.

Look at a tulip catalog.

Decide on colors and types of tulips.

Make sketch of flowerbed showing color patterns.

Figure out how many bulbs are needed and order them.

Prepare the soil with fertilizer.

Plant them at the right time in the fall.

Enjoy the flowers in the spring.

For a story about a summer adventure, your first list might look like this:

First time to the beach.

Eating fried fish and ice cream.

Tracking down the location where Marco might be imprisoned.

Finding a clue to the mystery.

Meeting two friends next door.

Asking about Marco Vitelli around town.

Learning to swim through the waves.

Leaving the dirty, hot city.

Sneaking in to free Marco and take him home.

Finding an abandoned sailboat, named *Sea Witch*.

Learning the mystery of the missing owner of the *Sea Witch*, Marco Vitelli.

Body surfing.

Visiting the Vitelli home and the belligerence of Madame Vitelli.

The vacation home we stayed in.

Organized by order of least to most important to the plot, the rearranged and trimmed list might run:

First time to the beach and the vacation home we stayed in.

Eating fried fish and ice cream.

Meeting two friends next door.

Learning to swim through the waves and body surfing.

Finding an abandoned sailboat, named *Sea Witch*.

Learning the mystery of the missing owner of the *Sea Witch*, Marco Vitelli.

Asking about Marco Vitelli around town with my friends.

Visiting the Vitelli home and the belligerence of Madame Vitelli.

Finding a clue to Marco's disappearance.

Tracking down the location where Marco might be imprisoned.

Sneaking in to free Marco and take him home.

With your simple outline, you have decided what to put in your story in what order without having written very much.

Now you are ready to start writing your story.

CHAPTER 3
Seven Writer's Skills

CHAPTER 3

Seven Writer's Skills

1. The Writer Discovers Subjects to Write About

A good writer finds subjects that are interesting and worth writing about. One develops a subject by putting ideas in focus, by developing a point of view. For comparison, think about focusing a camera, and the impact on a viewer of a focused picture versus a blurred one.

2. The Writer Senses an Audience

The writer keeps in mind those who will be reading each piece of writing. Who will the audience be? Is the intended piece right for the available audience? Will the readers understand it?

3. The Writer Uses Specifics

Show don't tell. Show your audience by using specific details that suggest an image to your reader. For example, compare these two passages, and notice the difference:

Whenever she frowned, the furrows on her face made her look old.

The frown lines were now permanently carved on her face, giving her the look of an ancient museum piece stored for centuries in the sub-basement.

4. The Writer Has in Mind the Effect Desired

Before writing, one decides on the effect the piece should create or the point it should make. Then the writer figures out how to accomplish this in the piece.

With the desired effect or point in mind, the writer can read the finished writing and ask, "Does it create the desired effect?" or "Does it get the point across?"

5. The Writer Writes

When writing, writers often begin to think out in detail for the first time what they have to say. Just get the thoughts written down on paper. Editing can be done later.

6. The Writer Develops a Critical Eye

The writer then becomes a ruthless reader, reading through the entire piece of writing with these questions in mind.

Does what is written make sense?

Is it clear and not hard to read or understand?

Is it written in terms that the reader understands?

Does it flow easily from the beginning to end?

7. The Writer Rewrites

The writer often revises any writing. One must rewrite until the piece is easy to read and understand.

Ensuring the voice, tense, pronoun use are consistent make writing clear and easy to read. Once a piece is finished, it can be reviewed to ensure it is consistent from beginning to end.

It can be particularly important to review the introductory paragraph(s). It should introduce the subject and the mood of the piece. Since the introduction is usually written when the story was first started, it can be reviewed once the story is complete to ensure it is still relevant. Then it can be revised if needed.

CHAPTER 4

Creating a Character

CHAPTER 4

Creating a Character

A **character** is a person in a story, novel, play, or film. The traits and qualities of this person define the character. Occasionally, animals or other creatures are characters, but they still have distinct qualities.

Readers will enjoy your stories if you create believable and likable characters. Although occasionally you'll also need to create a realistic but despicable villain for a story.

It is possible to create a portrait of a person, whether real or fictitious, using words. Words can suggest mental pictures. The right choice of words can suggest just the pictures you want your reader to have.

Here is an activity that will sharpen your skills in writing about characters.

1. In creating a character for a story, start by deciding what kind of personality the person has. Is the person pleasant or not? Good or evil? Outgoing or stand-offish? What is the first thing one notices about the personality of this character?

    For an exercise, look at someone you know and write down as many words as you can to describe his or her personality.

2. After you have figured out the personality, pay attention to the things the person has or does that make you think the person has the personality you are portraying.

   For example, what does this character have?

   Physical characteristics: fat/thin; short/tall; dark/light; old/young; sick/well, etc.

   Write some of these down.

   Clothing/possessions: expensive/cheap; well-kept/worn-out; clean/dirty; flashy/plain; large or small amounts; high quality/low quality; art or technology/no special possessions, etc.

   Write these down.

   What does this character do?

   Habits, mannerisms, deportment, gestures, expression, work habits, physical activity level.

   Write these down.

   How does this character treat people? What kinds of things does he or she say? How responsible is he or she? Can he or she be trusted?

   What deeds show this character's personality?

   Climbed a mountain, or stolen a car, painted a mural or graffiti on a building, or given away money to help others?

   Write these down.

3. Now decide how you are going to describe this character. This is a matter of how you see the character—your point of view or viewpoint. Is the character likable? Despicable? Pitiful? Funny?

4. Use the information you have gathered from steps 1–3 and write a description of this character.

5. Then check your work to see that what you say about the character is consistent. Does it like people one moment and hate them the next? Does it show a lot of integrity one day and none the next day? If this is the case, your character would be inconsistent and not very believable. Adequately develop the reasons your character might act a certain way, so it will behave consistently through the story.

    An actual example of an inconsistent character occurred when different writers contributed scripts to different episodes of the old television series "Star Trek." Some of the writers had Mr. Spock acting rather strangely. To eliminate this problem, the producers published a manual which gave character descriptions of all the main characters. That way they could maintain some uniformity of characterization from one script to the next, despite different authors.

6. Give your piece to others to read and find out what they get out of it. If it isn't what you intended, revise your description of the character and have others read it again and give you feedback

CHAPTER 5

Writing a Short Story

CHAPTER 5

Writing a Short Story

A work of fiction is not a real-life account but a product of an author's imagination. While it may contain many things that actually occurred, it is mainly made up.

Writing that tells a story is called a **narrative**. Narrate means *tell a story*. When you are recounting an event or sequence of events, it is a narrative piece.

The **short story** is a concise, fictional narrative that usually has only a few characters. The **novel** is a long fictional narrative. A collection of short stories may be printed in one book, while a novel usually occupies an entire volume.

Fictional narratives can be written about a wide range of subjects. For example, they can be romantic stories, science fiction, detective stories, historical fiction, adventure, and portraits of a personality. They normally have a main story line and sequence of events.

The greater length of the novel gives the writer greater freedom to explore and develop a plot and subplots than does the short story. Thus, the writer has the opportunity to involve more characters, develop subplots, and more fully describe characters and settings in a novel.

These elements are all useful in storytelling.

Narrator or storyteller: That could be the writer or a character in the story.

Plot: A story needs a plot. This means having a planned sequence of events that engages the reader and pulls them along. A story can start at the beginning and go to the end. It can also be effective to start in the middle or the most exciting or challenging part of the plot. Then the narrative can back up and tell how it was arrived at and resolved.

> *Suppose one is writing a story about an African adventurer. Let us say the plot is his journey into equatorial jungles in search of a surviving dinosaur that had been reported there. This is the plot—the main story line.*

Characters: Characters can be ordinary people, famous people, animals, elves, hobbits, even a robot. If the characters of your story are realistic and likable, they will carry the narrative forward. If the story lacks life, look at how well the characters in it have been given life.

Challenge: Characters in stories face challenges or barriers they need to overcome, or they face conflict or problems they need to solve. Without challenges or problems the reader can relate to, the narrative may not be engaging.

Setting and scenes: Any good story creates realistic settings and scenes the reader can feel a part of. Try to show, not tell about the settings.

> *In the story about the African jungle, one could tell about it:*

> *The jungle was hot and humid.*

Or one could show it:

> *The explorer pushed past leaves dripping with moisture and slogged along the muddy path. He was soon soaked in sweat and craving an ice-cold drink.*

Climax: Be sure the story has a climax or ending that makes reading the story worthwhile to the reader.

In learning to write fiction, it makes sense to start by writing short stories. The ability to craft an interesting story will eventually improve. With that, the length and complexity of plots and number of characters can increase. Then tackling a novel is certainly a possibility.

Here are some suggestions for the new, short story writer:

1. Read lots of stories by published writers. See how a professional writer does it.

2. Keep the story simple.

   a) Work out the plot and minimize the subplots. (Save subplots for longer stories.)

   b) Don't try to describe or develop too many characters. Stick to the main character(s). (You can develop more characters in longer stories.)

3. Try to stick to one point of view about the events of the story. (In a longer story you can show how a variety of different characters might look at the same events differently.)

Enjoy creating and writing your stories!

www.ingramcontent.com/pod-product-compliance
Lightning Source LLC
LaVergne TN
LVHW070057080426

835509LV00026B/3485